# How to Get Your Ex Back

*Strategies For Rekindling A Relationship With Your Ex, Even If They No Longer Have Romantic Emotions: Devious And Psychological Techniques To Persuade Your Ex That You Are Their Sole Ideal Partner*

**James Goodall**

# TABLE OF CONTENT

Impossible connections ........................................................ 1

LETTING YOUR EX KEEP GOING AND COMING BACK ON BOARD ................................................................... 4

YOUR BEST AWARD ............................................................ 23

SET OFF ON THE STAGE OF RE-ATTRACTION ........ 32

METHODS FOR QUICKLY GETTING YOUR WIFE BACK FOLLOWING A SEPARATION ............................ 59

Supporting Your Kids During A Separation Or Divorce ................................................................................ 69

Suppose it isn't amicable? ............................................... 95

WAYS TO MAKE YOUR RELATIONSHIP BETTER 101

The timing is crucial. ...................................................... 115

## IMPOSSIBLE CONNECTIONS

I'm a hopeless romantic at heart, so I'm hesitant to describe anything as "impossible" in this description. Love is stronger than most obstacles, and I would hate to rule out any truly amazing connection as unattainable.

On the other hand, some circumstances practically make meaningful relationships unthinkable. Sometimes, overcoming obstacles is necessary to make a romantic relationship succeed.

There are additional instances in which moving the earth is necessary for our presence.

However, there are situations where there is extremely little chance of accomplishment, and the task is more equivalent to relocating the entire cosmos.

As awful as it may sound, there are occasions when strange or uncontrollable situations dictate that we would be better off loving each other without a romantic relationship.

Aspire high and have faith in love. Don't let that belief cause you to lose sight of reality. Seldom do situations arise that are simply unsuitable for reviving a romance.

As the other female

I have a difficult predicament for you. Let's say you want your ex-boyfriend back, but he's got a serious relationship or is married to someone else. That poses a serious moral and practical problem.

Practically speaking, it's doubtful that attempts to mend a relationship under these situations will succeed. While it's possible to pull a man away from his spouse or significant other, it will undoubtedly be much harder than addressing a typical breakup scenario!

In addition, you should be aware that "the other woman" typically ends up losing things in the long run.

There are obviously exceptions, but generally speaking, relationships like this implode in an ugly way, leaving the "mistress" with a great deal of remorse, sorrow, and disgrace. She also rarely receives the entire attention of the man she desires.

From an ethical standpoint, you should consider whether making the man choose between you and commitment is truly appropriate.

# LETTING YOUR EX KEEP GOING AND COMING BACK ON BOARD

Every couple is reminded of the wonderful times they had in the past by these events, so it is understandable why your ex would be open to getting back to you. However, as they say, "You Must Go Slow." Furthermore, you at least feel that you are with each other because you love and understand each other. Joining the team makes space for a get-together and conversation.

The first thing you should know is that once you meet, you should never begin placing blame. Recall the best times you two can still share. Arrange for outings and walks in the outdoors as you mend your shared injuries. Make sure, particularly during this trying period, that you are not the victim of careless errors that you know annoy your partner.

Seeing Your Former Partner for the First Time After the Break

Your ex may desire you back if they try to meet with you. Your ex is attempting to examine unresolved feelings, at the very least. Above all, take your time and let things unfold naturally.

Try to propose a quick and sweet place for your ex to meet. Lunch or coffee will allow the reunion date to go swiftly and end before things get awkward, so both options are good. You want to introduce yourself to your ex in tiny doses at first. You'll always leave your ex wanting more of you if you don't give away too much and terminate the date fairly swiftly.

Additional Brilliant Strategies for Reuniting with Your Former Partner or Girlfriend

Reversing your breakup ultimately comes down to mindset. Additionally, it's about focusing on strategies to make your ex desire you again. There is a time and place for retreat strategies, fast reconnection tactics, and no-contact policies on the path to reconciliation. Ensure you understand what each of these terms means and what stage of the breakup you may be in. This makes it the ideal permission for your ex to return without any hassles.

## Taking Off the Rose-Tinted Glasses: You Can See Your Ex for Who He Is

First Activity

Make two lists of why you broke up when the two-week waiting period is up. It's crucial to put off doing this until you're feeling ready. If necessary, take more than two weeks. Your ideas will be a lot more objective and clear in this manner.

Split a piece of paper in half. Make a list of what your ex did that led to the split in one column. Make a list of everything you did in the other.

Put the two lists side by side for comparison. Look for connections. Were a few entries in one list responses to a specific action in the other?

Amy's lists might have looked something like this, for instance, if she had completed this exercise.

I was offended by Chris's demanding and domineering behavior.

We fought because I grew so sensitive to his domineering conduct and overreacted to things that never should have been a problem.

In a partnership, partners complement one another. They respond to one another's actions in ways that can potentially worsen negative emotional dynamics. Amy reacted badly to Chris's bad behavior. This played a part in the relationship's breakdown.

Notice the unfavorable ways the two of you responded to one another. When minor problems are overreacted, they become major ones.

Remember that this is not a blame-assignment exercise. Avoid being inclined to chastise or severely blame yourself for anything that you believe was your fault. These lists are meant to demonstrate that a tango requires two people. Every action has a response, and the emotional dynamic of the relationship is the result of both parties' efforts. Even the best people can exhibit their worst traits in a negative emotional situation.

Refer to these lists as you progress through the training over the next months. Every two to three weeks, go over them. Please feel free to add or modify them as your understanding of the relationship evolves.

Consider this: what could I have done differently?

You can think more clearly now that you've had some time to yourself and have regained emotional equilibrium. The background tensions and grievances from the partnership have had time to fade from your thoughts. It isn't screening your reactions to anything anymore.

In short, you are not the person you were on the day of the breakup.

Thus, consider how I would react to his actions differently now that I am in this position.

You could discover that your responses to these questions change each time as the weeks pass. You'll be shocked at how your viewpoint changes.

Who I Am, Who We Are

You will gain a better understanding of your relationship by completing this assignment.

You will be able to determine who in the relationship was putting in the most effort and who was finding it difficult to keep the connection going forward. More than that, you will learn more about your and your ex's personalities.

Why did the partnership have issues?

Was it because the two of you are so fundamentally unlike?

Or was it just one of you who wasn't putting in the effort or thinking enough to keep the relationship going?

To assist you in determining the next course of action, you have three options.

Are you two too dissimilar to be in a relationship? You might still believe that you are destined to be together and soulmates. However, it can be wise to acknowledge that you are essentially wrong for each other over time and start moving on if you realize that.

Was there a major issue in the relationship that you either did or did not do? It's not about blaming oneself again. Make an effort to see this as a chance for personal development. If you believe your actions were the primary cause of the issues in your relationship, it would be worthwhile to make changes and continue your efforts to win him back.

Was it something he did or didn't do that was the primary cause of the relationship's problems? Being frank with someone you love is difficult. But be as honest as you can as you write the list. And when you review it, consider each entry from his perspective, outlining the issues he brought about.

After looking through it, if you believe that the issues on his side of the list are:

Are they ones that you can live with in retrospect? "I can get over his tendency to forget significant dates."

Is it something that you can alter by altering who you are? "I know I can avoid that the next time; I was snappy when I didn't give him the space he needed."

Then, it makes sense to try to win him back once more.

Some inappropriate behavior, though, cannot be tolerated. Any signs of abuse—financial, sexual, physical, or emotional—indicate that it is not worthwhile to commit to this relationship.

You might believe that despite receiving harsh treatment, you only want to get your ex back. However, showing love to an abuser won't make them stop; in fact, it frequently serves to legitimize their violent actions.

See a trusted friend or a group that handles similar issues if you are unsure if you have been the victim of abuse. You are not suffering in silence. They will assist you in coming to a clear understanding.

The next stage is the same regardless of the outcome—whether it is better to end the relationship or continue attempting to get your ex back permanently.

Your ex was a significant figure in your life.

Are you the type of person that collaborated so effectively with your former partner?

You had duties, after all, and there were certain things your spouse handled without bothering you, but suddenly, you're left to deal with things on your own.

In situations like this, you might not be over your ex just because they were a necessary part of your day-to-day existence.

You might want to stand back and consider your options if this describes you.

Your former partner may have played a valuable and helpful role in your life, and naturally, the emptiness they left behind can always serve as a reminder of the split. But you must figure out how to step into those positions and deal with life.

As an illustration

If your former partner was the household's "breadwinner," you must start a business or hunt for employment if you don't already have one to make ends meet.

If he constantly replaces the oil in the automobile, you should plan routine maintenance for your car so you won't have to worry about it.

Alternatively, if you can't bear to cook for yourself without remembering how it used to be because your ex used to prepare everything for you while they were present, then temporarily switch to a convenient meal.

You likely won't be able to fulfill every role they performed in your life—especially the job of emotional support—but you may still assist yourself by taking small steps towards simplifying your life.

Try not to even attempt to take up the entire load at once.

Low regard for oneself

As mentioned in point 3, low self-esteem is the concern that one will never find someone like them again.

And it's a serious concern.

People find it difficult to let go of the familiar because they are accustomed to it.

First of all, as social animals, we are. It can be difficult for you to let go of someone or people, even if they are not the right fit for you.

A study by the London School of Economics revealed that having strong relationships and mental health were more important for happiness than riches.

You secretly think that no one will ever be as good as your ex—if not better. You would prefer to make things right or find a way to reconcile, but the truth is that you cannot make someone rethink their decision to tap out.

You still lack closure.

It's conceivable that your ex abruptly ended things with you or ghosted you without explaining.

Thus, you haven't received the resolution you require to go on.

Getting closure for any life-changing event, be it in a relationship, career, or other domain, is critical.

Finality is the result of closure. In other words, letting go of the past.

Honoring the transition away from what's finished to something new," psychiatrist Abigail Brenner wrote in Psychology Today.

However, to do this, you must accept responsibility for your choices, lament the loss, cry if necessary, and create plans for the near future.

These will compel you to alter for the better and get on with your existence.

Not being able to grieve.

We may be stuck with ex-partners who no longer serve us in large part because we don't give ourselves enough time to grieve properly.

We often dive straight into a new relationship or a million projects that distract us from facing up instead of dealing with the deep pool of weighty feelings that a breakup inspires.

Naturally, this may seem to work for a while, but ultimately, things begin to slow down, stop, or even completely cease.

And when they do, those unresolved, unpleasant feelings again rear their ugly heads, dragging your ex along with them.

You suffer from Repetition Compulsion.

According to psychologist and therapist Perpetua Neo, "Repetition compulsion is the reason why your past relationships can influence your new ones."

What is meant by that?

We often feel obligated to make up for a mistake that occurred in a previous relationship. The main issue is that we might pick or be among people unwilling or unable to change.

Most of the time, we are unaware of this compulsion.

Moving on from an ex is difficult if you feel obligated to make up for a transgression from your previous relationship.

Not enough time has elapsed.

Naturally, this is the most straightforward explanation for accepting heartbreaks that anyone can come up with.

Maybe "too little time has gone by since your heart broke."

You might need longer than you anticipate if the connection is long-lasting.

You have many habits and patterns you acquired during the relationship, after all. It might be incredibly difficult to adapt when you're abruptly put in a new position.

It's like losing a piece of oneself.

Reaching out to your former partner (or the other way around)

My buddy, if you're still making a lot of effort to get in touch with your ex, or if you find yourself thinking about getting in touch with them or them reaching out to you, you still need to get over something quickly.

Furthermore, it's a terrible idea, in particular, if the relationship was abusive.

I'll tell you what: the need for contact is a sign of the need for connection. And after a relationship ends, the connection needs to be resolved.

In addition to trauma bonding, which makes you feel alive only when you are assaulted, you can be in constant distress due to excessive communication with your toxic ex or them reaching out to you.

You don't need to know about their new pals or how their day went if your main concern is keeping yourself sane.

Establishing sound boundaries is essential to move past the relationship and find healing.

Continuous thinking back

Do you think about your ex all the time?

What about the enjoyable time you two had together?

Or maybe you find yourself thinking about the decisions and statements you made before before the split all the time, or you find yourself regretting every little error you two have made.

Well, you haven't moved on if you dwell on details of your ex-partner or split. It's difficult to avoid mentally reliving the past most of the time.

You may be dwelling on the problem to come up with a solution. Or maybe you're just looking for approval from people in your immediate vicinity since you feel like a victim.

According to a 2008 study, meditating or thinking about an ex-lover nonstop is frequently linked to rejection.

Contemplations such as "If only we had wanted the same thing out of the relationship," "If only the fun, good times had lasted longer," and "If only this...if only that!" could cause people to dwell over regrets."

Unhealthy relationships nearly always have happy times as well, which at the time gave us hope that everything would work out in the partnership, to regrets and unfulfilled dreams following a breakup.

After a breakup, it's very simple to go into a blaming spiral, yet doing so is counterproductive to our real healing and development.

A breakup is simply a shift, and life happens, and that's okay.

From the inside, I realize that it can be difficult to perceive or accept.

However, it becomes simpler to point the finger of blame and criticism at your partner, yourself, or anybody else who could ease your agony.

While dwelling on guilt may boost your ego, it hinders your ability to move past it.

And once more, showing that you're still deeply connected to the past by losing yourself in daydreams about the positive aspects of your ex or in memories of your time together.

This pattern is frequently linked to anxiety or despair. This can make it difficult for you to recognize and process your emotions as you make a great effort to focus on the circumstance rather than your feelings.

### A needless and never-ending comparison

Comparisons can be highly damaging, particularly if they reference a previous relationship or an ex.

Comparing your new relationship or circumstances to those of your ex regularly may indicate that you haven't fully processed all of the emotions you still associate with those former experiences.

To be honest, moving past your ex involves evaluating the experiences in your life on their own merits rather than the merits of someone who is no longer a part of it.

Consider it.

## The act of cyberstalking

Even after your relationship with your ex was publically ended, you still have feelings for them if you're stalking them online.

It can be problematic in and of itself that social media has made it simpler for people to stay in touch with people they know.

It demonstrates that you are still overly invested when you check your ex's social media page and search for evidence of their newfound life, including places they go and people they meet.

Additionally, it demonstrates that your ex still occupies a significant amount of space in your heart and, naturally, mind, leaving little to no place for recovery, development, and stronger bonds.

## mourning the unrealized promise of your partnership

Shannon Thomas, a writer and licensed therapist, stated, "people grieve over the potential that was in their past relationships."

our unfulfilled aspirations and expectations for our potential relationship with that other. All the dreams and ambitions we shared that were never fulfilled. Our idle fantasies are fed by the persistent "if only..." thoughts.

This frequently happens even when you're not conscious of it since the ideas seep into our subconscious.

## YOUR BEST AWARD

After reuniting and making it official, what comes next?

You need to know one thing at the end of your second date: you need to spend the night together again following the kiss that ends this date.

Together, you will awaken in shock and, maybe, relief that things worked out as they did. Right now, this might be the most beautiful day of your life. You should also be pleased with yourself because you've found the love of your life again.

You all need to stay in bed a little longer and, most importantly, share your first (essential) meal as the morning starts. You should spend the morning of your first official meeting together. Check the amount of food available now (the day before). A full menu includes items like bacon, bread, croissants, coffee, juice, and eggs. The amount of food you provide for your partner demonstrates your importance to them. This will give the impression that you are giving and create a cozy, feel-good atmosphere around you (you know how food makes people feel).

Make sure you remain in unison the entire time. Now is the moment to compensate for the years, months, or weeks you have lost apart. Make sure you haven't discussed any commitments or intentions yet. Telling them how much you've missed them is the only thing you should say to them.

It's official—you two are back together after spending this weekend together.

-The recent pledges

It will take around six or seven days for the relationship to strengthen. It will also be necessary to make some new commitments. Since you already know one another, the commitments must be made as soon as you get back together, sometimes within a week. This is to ensure that you avoid repeating your previous mistakes.

-Let's start by acknowledging that, at first, you all probably didn't have any plans and made a lot of blunders. Instead of blaming one another, you should be self-assured and mature enough to acknowledge that perhaps you are all responsible for each other's actions and that you should go on to make new beginnings.

-Get rid of the so-called "no string attached lovers" and the few "not that serious flings." They must leave. It makes no difference if you haven't spoken to them in weeks because you are back with your former partner. Make sure you and your former partner eliminate them quickly and efficiently, with each of you on the other's side. A month into a serious relationship, it's never nice to have one of them contact you and call you ¡§honey¡¨ or ¡§sweetheart¡¨ while your partner looks at you and feels suspicious. If you encounter one of them in person one day, that shouldn't occur either.

-Discuss your expectations for this relationship, including your goals and the nature of the collaboration.

Finally, the following suggestions can assist you in making your new partnership work:

- Acquire compromise skills. From now on, you should agree that people shouldn't impose themselves or their viewpoints; instead, discussions and agreements should always occur before making decisions.

-Justify your agreement: Essentially, the idea is that, in the end, you should always have the fortitude to forgive one another, regardless of disagreements.

-Build trust: Maybe it's time for you to change if you don't trust your partner because they are too attractive or secretive. You can never be incorrect if you have enough trust. When your partner makes judgments you trust, things in your relationship will move forward and improve. In a relationship, trust is like an exercise in brainstorming; you never come out of it a loser—rather, you are just improving your odds of doing better.

-Give your romantic life a little kick. It is essential to have sex, and it will only make your partner feel wonderful about the union. A very healthy and abundant sexual life boosts the confidence of a desired man or woman. Thus, don't be afraid to engage in foreplay, wear knickers or Converse, or express your individual preferences.

-Finally, but just as importantly, divide up financial duties. One can never say enough about it. However, in terms of money, your spouse is also able to do for you what you can do for them. Ladies, if your partner frequently buys you presents, make sure you return the favor. And males, please show your partner your appreciation by taking her to a spa or on a cruise one of these days if she is kind enough to lend you financial support occasionally.

A relationship—even one you've lost and gained back—needs willpower and fresh blood. Never assume that the relationship will work out on its own just because you have someone's back.

## CHAPTER 2: WHAT CAUSED THE DISPUTE?

Using cause and effect is one of the most popular problem-solving techniques. Breakups are by no means an anomaly. Whatever the problem is, figuring out what kind of problem it is is always the best place to start. As for your split, you should begin by determining what went wrong. You might want to try writing it down for future reference.

Considerations For Ascertaining The Cause Of A Breakup

True, the subheading sounds more like the section title of a thesis paper, but that's a positive thing. Although it can be challenging, analyzing a broken relationship is essential to win your ex back. You must find a way to let the past go, look at the big view, and grow from your mistakes.

Sincerity

This is an excellent issue to consider when trying to figure out why a relationship ended. Being objective and truthful about what truly happened and you are too emotionally invested in the regrettable event of the breakup to think logically. Keep in mind that you don't have to place blame for your partner's breakup simply because you understand why. That is not true at all. It's not important to figure out who was mistaken. Rather, concentrating on how you could do better the next time necessitates being forthright and truthful about the real reason behind your split.

It makes sense that since a romantic relationship comprises two people, the topic of your partner's contribution to the stability of your union will also come up. Remember to present things positively and be honest about your partner's role in improving your relationship.

As an illustration

You will spend extra time with your partner to show them how much you care.

False: You will work less hours so that you may spend more time with your partner.

Even if your goal and strategy may be synonymous, how you achieve them might make things better for you and your ex. Of course, your ex is also exposed to the same.

Your spouse will indeed grow to comprehend your feelings. Your partner will not treat you disrespectfully, despite what you may believe.
In other words, it is possible to be polite and sincere simultaneously.

Give each other the benefit of the doubt when discussing or considering the reason for your breakup, and avoid using hurtful language.

Finalization

Splits don't always result from mutually agreed-upon decisions. At times, it can be completely biased. If you were the one who was left in the dark and perplexed after the separation, you must first find closure. Hopefully, your former partner will willingly support you in your journey forward. If not, you can choose to either move on from the split or try to determine what went wrong on your own. Either way, you should keep your thoughts about your ex-partner neutral. That's not the place to start if you're looking for reconciliation.

## SET OFF ON THE STAGE OF RE-ATTRACTION

You must give this delicate stage your whole attention. You will have to begin the process of attempting to win your ex back over again if you make a mistake at this point. But if you do this correctly, you will speak with your former partner shortly. You need to get in touch with your ex throughout the re-attraction phase.

Make contact

If you want to be with your ex again, contact her. Keep in mind that this only applies if you are dumped. Sending them nasty messages to tell them how much they upset you is inappropriate now. It's inappropriate to bombard them with texts or phone calls. This is not the moment to project neediness or desperation. You should consider carefully what you want to say to your former partner. Contacting your ex can be done in several ways. These are the following:

SMS

For individuals who wish to win their ex back, texting has shown to be a very successful strategy. Give your ex a short text message to cheer them up and provide useful information. You should text your ex to let them know, for instance, that you noticed the sale sign and recalled how much they love sales if you know they appreciate them. I wish them a happy day. End the SMS message. Stay away from telling your ex to text you back.

Making a Call

It takes more work to make a call than to text. This is because the sound of your voice will reveal to your ex how you are feeling. If you plan to call your ex, you must remain composed.

An email or letter

You might write your ex a letter as an alternative to communicating or texting them. Apply the same logic you would if you were messaging or texting someone. Write a brief, non-intrusive note. Don't start chatting about your relationship or introducing yourself. Make it useful and uncomplicated.

You ought to use caution when speaking with your ex. Don't call each other by the "pet names" you used to call each other. You should avoid acting too casually. Avoid using terms like "sweetie" and "babe." Simply use the individual's name. You should use your discernment to determine the best course of action based on how your ex responds to you. Your ex will likely call or text you back if you don't put them on the spot.

Establish a date.

In this context, "date" refers to an activity or outing you wish to take your ex on that might lead to a satisfying outcome in the bedroom or anywhere else. Choose an activity you and your ex-partner will likely enjoy in advance. The activity should be sufficiently "neutral" to ensure your date feels at ease. Ensure that you:

Avoid using the word "date."

When discussing a joint activity with your ex, you must be cautious in your language. The word "date" will raise suspicions since your ex will link it to specific behaviors you engaged in throughout your dating relationship. Never mention or reference previous outings you or your ex may have gone on. Don't try to replicate such experiences.

Avoid making out with other people.

Avoid the foolish mistake of making your ex jealous by flirting with other people. Relationships have never benefited from flirting. Indeed, it's frequently mentioned as one of the causes of partnership arguments. Your ex will reject your attempts to get closer if you flirt with others since they interpret it as a bad sign.

Pay attention, but don't go overboard.

You want to pay close attention to your ex without bothering her throughout the "date." Engage and involve your former partner in the discussion without placing them under duress.

Reintroducing your ex to everything that first drew them to you is the goal of your outing. When your ex sees you, she'll think of happy times and memories that you bring back. You should exercise caution not to appear overly eager to set up another date after a successful one. After a date, always go for the kiss; if she doesn't return the favor, just smile and carry on. Even though it might be too soon for her, remember that you will succeed the next time. After a week, plan your next date.

Reestablish your bond.

Getting back together with your ex is not insurmountable. If you put in the work, you can accomplish anything. When you get back together, you must be careful not to become overconfident. If you have unsolved concerns, you can break up again after your previous breakup. You must address the problems that caused the breakup. For your relationship to get stronger, you must also rebuild it. You ought to:

Handle pressure from both the inside and the outside.

Pressures from the outside and inside affect relationships. Your relationship may suffer as a result of your insecurities. Your relationship could be challenging because of your friends and families. Regarding your relationship, you need to set limits and work on yourself. Address issues rather than putting them under the rug.

Develop closeness

Your actions and words towards your spouse can foster relationship intimacy. Emotional connection is crucial since your spouse should know your thoughts, desires, wants, needs, and ambitions. It's crucial to have physical closeness since it shows your partner that you are interested in them. It is important to acknowledge the power of touch. Touches that appear harmless are a good way to develop intimacy.

Develop your ability to communicate clearly.

Your relationship will be saved if you learn excellent communication techniques. Conflict and miscommunication are frequently the results of poor communication. Speaking your mind and hearing your partner out are both components of communication. This needs to be handled with decency. Don't be scared to voice your thoughts, and keep an open mind to those of others.

Address the dispute

Not avoiding disagreement but learning how to handle it well is the key to happy partnerships. It's important to settle disputes in a way that makes both of you feel respected and happy. Acquire the skill of fair combat. Avoid holding things in until they blow up. Take a seat and talk about the issues at hand. Remember that you are a group. Resolving a dispute benefits you both.

Continue to be passionate.

Don't expect it to burn brightly if you don't work to fan the fires in your love life. Talking about what works, what doesn't, and potential additions to your sex life is important between you and your partner. Instead of focusing on weakness, emphasize who you are. Saying "I love it when you..." will make your partner feel good about themselves and encourage them to do the activity more often.

A sound partnership grows more robust over time. This is a result of you two learning what functions well and poorly. You get older, learn to value one another and learn to protect what you have. But that doesn't mean you have to stop doing the small things that make your relationship meaningful as time goes on. You have a plethora of options for improving your relationship. Don't forget to notice the small things, even when you make big gestures. Your partnership is significant. Take good care of it.

8. Take a Date

Don't become too agitated. Simply attempt to go on a date. Going on a date does not always imply committing. It's just lunch or supper with a potential friend. A casual date could be quite beneficial in this situation. Your ex will undoubtedly lose it when they discover you went on a date. Your ex will undoubtedly miss you. They will be deeply hurt by the possibility of losing you to someone else! Recall that your most powerful tool is jealousy.

Additionally, it demonstrates your confidence. You're prepared to take on the world because you have faith in yourself. When you receive compliments from others, you'll feel more assured. You'll instantly start to feel confident in your attractiveness, which is a given. You require this confidence.

If it's not a date, you can meet new acquaintances. Getting to meet new individuals is always enjoyable.

Imagine your former partner is seeing someone else. Never worry about anything. Keep your cool. Your former partner is likely looking for a second chance. Long-term success is not achieved in rebound relationships. Under no circumstances should you call him or her out of jealousy! Even your ex might benefit from a connection. This is because he or she will forget all the unpleasant memories that accompanied the breakup and instead recall the enjoyable times spent with you.

Give it some time if you're still not convinced. You will be the one to view the outcomes.

9. Light the Fire Again

It's time to reestablish contact with your ex after you were able to ignore them for a few weeks. Whether or not they desired to get in touch with you during the "no contact" time is irrelevant. Just keep in mind that all you have to do to get in touch with your former partner again is construct a bridge.

In a typical scenario, you two would most likely be attending a party where one of you would have run into the other. You two would have swapped phone numbers and spoken for a few hours. After that, you would begin messaging. Your phone would beep periodically, giving you a tingling sensation. You two go on a couple of dates. And just like that, you two are living together and in a relationship.

But you guys already know each other intimately in this case. Which pants does he or she wear to bed? You know. You are aware of your ex's vices. Every detail about you is known to your ex. How can you draw in someone of such caliber? Yes, you make fun of them.

Rather than calling your ex, you should initiate contact with them via text. In contrast to a text, which seems extremely informal, a phone call can span hours. Some things you should keep in mind are

• Avoid coming out as clingy and desperate when texting.

• If your ex isn't responding to your SMS immediately, stop sending them.

• Avoid focusing too much on a tedious subject. It should be humorous and engaging to read. Your ex should be the topic of conversation, not you. Put a stop to the conversation immediately if you feel that it is becoming dull. Don't let the conversation drag because it will seem that you're interested in speaking with your ex. You must give them the impression that you are content and have outgrown their presence.

Your text should primarily aim to establish a channel of contact. This is not the time for a long-distance discussion. Your ex must be left wanting more from you. Thus, a text message stating, "Hey, just passed your favorite ice cream parlor," should be effective. Your ex will likely respond to you. It's possible that your ex won't text back right away. Your abrupt text will perplex them because, having not spoken to each other, your ex will undoubtedly miss you and gladly respond. Keep the discussion focused and brief. Make sure you leave them wanting more when you close the chat!

After sending the first text, how long will it take to send the second? The next day, you are not allowed to text your ex. If you text them, your ex will know you are waiting to chat with them all day. Therefore, refrain from texting for a couple of days.

Respond casually if your former partner texts you first. Don't let the fact that your ex texted you get you too thrilled. You must maintain your composure.

Most people make the error of simply going back to their ex-partners after mending their relationship. They never stop phoning or contacting their former girlfriend or boyfriend. Conversely, you must make fun of your ex. Your former partner needs to be anxious to get your texts! You will win this war in this manner.

After contacting your ex for a week or two, you can finally set up a meeting. But since this is your last performance, you must be extremely conscious of your body language. Meeting your ex face-to-face can be challenging because you'll need to think of quick answers and reactions. Your ex will see your posture and movements.

When you see your former partner, you need to exude confidence. You look good and are in good shape by now. With your fresh look, you can entice your ex. Your ex will be impressed. There's no way your ex can hold out against you. When you are with your ex, keep your eyes on them. This will demonstrate your concern and lack of intimidation. Engage in lighthearted discussion instead of bringing up painful recollections from the past. The moment will be ruined for you both by unpleasant recollections. You can talk about enjoyable memories, for sure. Throughout the talk, try to maintain your distance. After listening to your ex, end the encounter. Make a lunch for a different day.

Signs will be thrown at you by your ex. There's a good possibility your ex is eager to get back together if they consent to another meeting. You must immediately realize that you are getting close to your objective if you see that your ex has dressed to impress you.

You must make a little more fun of your ex to win big. Don't start a physical connection with your former partner. Sure, it will be really alluring. Even though you truly want to kiss your ex during the farewells, resist the urge.

Develop a close relationship during each meeting. At the second meeting, lightly touch his or her hands. In the upcoming meeting, lightly touch your ex's thighs with your hands. Don't forget to take your dates to public areas. Stay away from flats altogether. Go out to eat or watch a movie as though you are only now getting to know your former partner. And most of all, go slowly.

I'm not talking to my ex, so should I respond to his text?

Generally speaking, you shouldn't reply to your ex's SMS while you're not in contact. Psychotherapist Samantha Rodman says that if your ex is messaging you, it's likely because they are thinking back on the relationship and possibly even missing you. However, texting your ex might lead to emotional regression and possibly impede aspects of the healing process.

Remember that the no-contact rule's goal is to heal and transform into a person your ex would want to spend time with again. Furthermore, you are merely diverting your attention if you reply to your ex's texts every time they do.

Should I take my ex's call while we're not talking?

No. You ought not to take your ex's call. This only doesn't apply if you are about to break off your no-contact period and are already content with your life. Don't answer their call if you believe speaking with your ex will make you feel more obsessed with them.

And what if, in the interim, my ex moves on?
What happens if my ex-partner marries someone and they don't communicate?
What happens if I go cold turkey with my ex?

Excellent inquiries. And to each of them, the response is NO, they won't.

They won't be able to move on so fast if you and your ex had a significant connection. Maintaining no communication would just increase their longing for you and remind them of your positive traits. This is where you have to take a chance. Being a weirdo and constantly texting and stalking your ex is the alternative to having no contact, and it will most likely result in a restraining order being placed against you. There's not much of a choice.

Why can't I shorten the no-contact period? For a few days or a week, maybe?

So you want to stop sending your ex so many texts for a few days just to start sending them again a few days later?

No.

After a breakup, it takes some time for people to start missing their exes and get rid of bad memories.

You must offer it to them.

More significantly, you need to improve yourself to become a happier and more self-assured individual.

Your ex cannot persuade themselves to get back together with you unless you transform yourself for the better.

What Happens If My Ex and I Have Kids?

You must have little contact if you are a parent. This implies that you should only contact your former partner when essential.

You only talk to them about significant issues or your kids.

You don't discuss any private matters. When your ex inquires about something personal, you respond by saying something like,

"I'm not ready to talk to you about my life yet. I sincerely hope you can understand and limit the discussion to our child or children.

What would happen if I moved in with my ex?

If you live together, it will be difficult to avoid contact and give each other some space. For this reason, however, I strongly advise you to discover a means of moving out for the time being.

Tell your ex that you're having trouble living with them, and I'd like to move out for a while. Inform them that you will decide on your living situation later when you have more clarity.

If moving out isn't an option, you should have little interaction. Don't talk about anything personal; only communicate with your ex if it's vital. Create a space in the house only for you, and only occupy it.

My ex believed I wasn't committed to them or gave them enough attention. Wouldn't they want to go on and feel like I don't care if I didn't communicate with them?

For those who didn't put enough effort into maintaining the relationship, that is a serious cause for concern. But with the separation, they want to work harder.

You've already attempted to persuade them that this time will be different if you read this book. I hope that you'll be more dedicated and make an attempt. That you'll be considerate.

Furthermore, it was unsuccessful.

Your ex believes you are doing all this because you fear losing them, which is why it didn't work. Because you are desperate and in need, you are demonstrating your concern. And maintaining contact with them validates that conviction.

Your former partner believes you'll resume your previous behavior after you get them back.

The easiest approach to assist them in getting past this misconception is to demonstrate to them that you are no longer in need of anything by making no contact.

Moving on and not losing interest in them does not imply this. That indicates that you are spending some time identifying your problems and determining how to solve them.

When trying to persuade them after you've cut off communication, your earnest attempt to reflect and find a solution to your problems will be very effective.

What will happen if I don't talk to my ex for a month or two?

That is a valid query.

Well, that's not a very good question.

That's one of the things your racing thoughts will probably query.

As I mentioned before, we can never know what is going through someone else's mind. If we are not mind readers, then no.

However, I can tell you what typically occurs to an ex-partner when communication ceases following a split.

Your ex never really had to deal with the breakup if you two have been in continual communication following it. Yes, they decided to end your relationship, and they most likely believed it was right.

But because you continued acting like they still had you, they were never truly faced with the breakup.

A breakup entails the loss of a loved one. Furthermore, they never really went through the breakup if they never felt like they lost you.

They never experienced grief or that sinking black hole sensation in the pit of their stomachs.

When you stop communicating, there's a strong likelihood that your ex will become distraught. It is another different to discuss how people respond to that grief.

They may begin to reach out to you daily.
They could become enraged.
They may become completely indifferent to you and shut down. (Most of the time, this is just temporary, so relax and tell your racing mind to stop.)
They may begin following you on social media or through mutual acquaintances.

They may even put their breakup behind them and focus on getting well.

They may show signs of interest in you by reaching out to you on a casual basis to find out about your activities. In other words, they will throw you a bone. They will also realize that you are still their pet and that they have complete control over you if you take it.

**Case Study:** No Contact made her ex crazy for her. But not in a good way.

# METHODS FOR QUICKLY GETTING YOUR WIFE BACK FOLLOWING A SEPARATION

This time, your wife is sincere in her desire to end the marriage, and it appears that this is her final decision. Perhaps someone has moved out already. Despite your best efforts, she remains resolute in her pursuit of a divorce.

How do you proceed? How do you get her to reconsider? Can your marriage be saved, and if so, how?

In the last year alone, I have directly assisted over one thousand guys through a separation.

Observing these men, I've found that those who could keep their marriage intact tended to employ a similar tactic. I will provide an overview of this method in this short book.

I'll then demonstrate how to use it for you. Then, by reading the pages below, you can obtain more specific instructions. There are three steps to the fundamental strategy.

**Step 1:** Give up on your desperation and concentrate on the things under your control.

**Step 2:** Decide which man you want to be and then try to become that man.

**Step 3:** Take every chance to show your wife this man. This is the challenging part.

Getting your wife back to trust you is your top priority in this whole situation. I refer to this separation approach as the "three plus one" because of this. Three steps lead to a single car.

Both sides of the equation are necessary. In a moment, we'll go into further detail about why trust reconstruction is crucial in addition to that. Let's first go over these three processes in more depth.

The 3+1 Method for Regaining Your Wife's Trust

**Step 1:** Give up on your desperation and concentrate on the things under your control. Although these two stages may seem distinct initially, they work best when combined like a pair of gloves. Doing one entails doing the other. Why? Because attempting to control an uncontrollable situation leads to desperation.

Focusing on what you can truly control and making the most of it is the natural response to desperation. Since you cannot complete the tasks, this must be the first step in your plan. You won't have the best opportunity to save your marriage if you can't restrain yourself.

It's similar to how everyone usually tells you to wear your oxygen mask before aiding others—including your family—on an airplane. This is because if you're losing control yourself, you won't be able to properly assist your family. Until you prove to your wife that you are capable of happiness, she will never believe you can make her happy.

Thus, pay attention to the things under your control. Your actions, your words, your thoughts,

your disposition—all of it—and then worry later about the other side of things, your wife's side of things.
That may seem paradoxical, but that is the way this process needs to begin. Quit being desperate and concentrate on the things you can control. This takes us to the second step: decide who the guy you want to be and then set out to become him. Your wife is beyond your control. Here, there are no magical mysteries. Your wife can only choose to return to the marriage if she so chooses, and only then will she be able to give it her all. by herself.

Although you can't force her to choose, you can give her a strong incentive. It may sound corny, but self-improvement is a straightforward way to do this. To do this, identify the type of spouse you know you can be and put in the effort to develop into that man right now. You might be able to see into the past. Think back to when your relationship first began. Your union. And you'll realize that this man was once you. You were a better spouse once. You may need to rehabilitate this man because you used to watch out for your wife. Alternatively, some of you may know you haven't fulfilled your potential as a husband. This is the appropriate moment. It's time to get serious and put your best foot forward.
It's time to look at yourself in the mirror and decide what type of man you want to see there. This is when leadership, patience, forgiveness, and

selfless love become relevant. It's time to grind your teeth, regain your composure, reclaim your masculinity, and go to work.

Turn into the man you know you should be. For this discussion, let's suppose that you already know the kind of man you want to be and that you have changed for the better to become a better father and husband. For many men, this is the conclusion of the procedure. They know one more vital step is left, but this is as far as they can go.

**Step 3:** Act to improve your wife's life by demonstrating that guy to her. This is the hardest stage in the plan, as we mentioned at the beginning of the chapter. Merely implementing the modifications discussed in Step 2 is insufficient. You need to demonstrate those improvements to your wife in a way that works. In a manner that prompts her to consider the new you.

This sometimes entails intensifying your household responsibilities, taking on greater fatherly responsibilities, chasing your spouse, and demonstrating your undeniable desire for her. Sometimes, this implies the exact opposite. It may be the case that giving your wife exactly what she wants may completely defy her expectations and prove to her that you have truly changed.

Airspace!

Keep a distance from her until she is ready to come to you, at least for a short while. This makes it clear why step three is the most difficult in the plan since, in contrast to phases two and three, your approach to step three will be completely customized to your situation and separation. Why? Because both your wife and you are exceptional human beings. You all have distinct personalities. Your partnership is distinct. Your talks, issues, situations, and past are uniquely yours.

Yes, the majority of separations indeed have a similar structure. Most men who visit the Haven will encounter comparable difficulties and roadblocks in their quest to return to fulfilling marriages. They'll stumble into similar situations in the future. To help you avoid the most typical mistakes men make while divorcing, I have prepared the final chapter as a bonus. It will ultimately be up to you to work out and maximize the specifics of the day-to-day operations. And here, my friends, is where we return to the main objective—rebuilding trust—that we discussed at the outset. Rebuilding trust is the main objective of each of these three processes. This may seem like a daunting endeavor, and it truly is. But remember that there is a straightforward equation for determining trust: reliability plus consistency plus time.

Rebuilding trust takes time. You gradually rebuild it. A single brick at once. You see, your wife no longer has faith in you. She's been wounded, left with scars, and has fortified her heart with walls. She will, therefore, initially react with skepticism, mistrust, and possibly even fury when she sees you making adjustments in step two.

# Benefits of Having a Boyfriend or Girlfriend in Chapter Two

"Love is the desire to give everything one has in order to support the spiritual development of another person or oneself."
M. Scott Peck

In this chapter, I'll discuss the advantages of having a girlfriend or boyfriend in your life. Having someone to spend time with is crucial regardless of whether you end up with your ex. More than ever, our generation must experience more love and less selfishness.

In a healthy relationship, you can have stability and consistency. Having plenty of love partners texting you on your phone may seem more intriguing and enjoyable, but trying to satisfy them all causes much more stress. If possible, you ought to find someone else to spend your attention on or try to win your ex back. Here are some explanations for why it could be ideal for you to locate a life partner:

Inspiration

Having a partner, whether a boy or a girl, can improve your stability in general. People's behaviors are motivated by their romantic desires. You can focus more on the things you enjoy doing, like your career, dream job, or any other interests you may have if you have a girlfriend or boyfriend.

After you've been together for a while, you start talking to your spouse more about your views and future. Why? When someone other than yourself finally shows you care. You now have someone else who can support and assist you on your trip into the future since you are in a healthy relationship. A good partner will support you no matter what, help you achieve your goals, and ensure you stay on course. They can help guys stay more focused and grounded since they are mature. In a relationship, you are responsible for encouraging your partner in all of their endeavors.

adoration

You obtain the most significant thing you require in a connection. And love is that. You are prospering because of love, not because of accomplishments or recognition. Love is a given in partnerships that are in good health. We frequently lose sight of the beauty of loving and being loved in such situations, especially when committed to someone. Try your hardest not to allow this to happen to you. There is no other way to experience true love but via relationships.

Happiness

Giving is one of the most powerful aspects of being in a relationship. I think a partnership cannot truly exist without giving, whether it's a smile and some love or some time, money, or attention. In sincere interactions, the only things visible are gifts and joyful giving. We often assume that when we think about ourselves alone, we overlook the joy of giving. As soon as we consider others before ourselves, life is great.

Your Life Will Be More Meaningful

Individuals who have established strong romantic bonds with others discover that their lives have far greater significance. It t's true that a lot of us view relationships as the most paramount aspect of our lives. They greatly enrich our lives and motivate us to continue living and progressing.
You do not consider what you have accomplished with your life when you are nearing the end of it. You take all those achievements and that prestigious or wealthy status for granted. When it comes down to it, it all becomes worthless; we really want to be surrounded by people who love and care about us. Relationships will ultimately be the only thing that counts in life. Thus, you should always be working towards building them.

Extended Lifespan

Several scientific studies have demonstrated that those in romantic partnerships have a higher chance of living longer than those in single relationships. People's lifestyles seem to make sense after someone else walks in, which could be one explanation.

Increased Income

Although it's not a good incentive to go into a relationship, one advantage of being in one is that it will eventually make you wealthier overall. In a partnership, having two sources of income can also provide some flexibility if one spouse needs to divide their time between working and taking care of the family or kids.

Steer clear of loneliness.

The obvious benefit of having a long-term relationship is that loneliness is avoided. A lifetime of loneliness can break your spirit. You are more prone to have depressing situations in your life if you feel lonely. You can wish to resolve to get your ex back or find a new relationship if you don't want to deal with such emotions in your life.

Decreased Stress

Almost everyone has some level of stress at some point in their relationship. However, generally speaking, having a second companion can make our lives more peaceful. Relationships involve more than just sharing responsibilities; they also involve times when we can lower our stress levels by supporting and believing in each other.

## Supporting Your Kids During A Separation Or Divorce

When parents divorce, a child may go through a great deal of sadness in addition to confusion, wrath, and uncertainty. To assist your kids in dealing with the breakup, as their parents, you may offer them consistency and reassure them by positively responding to their needs.

Speak With Others About Help
Support from others is necessary for recovery following a breakup or divorce. It won't help if you try to spend this time alone, even though you might want to. Do not try to solve this by yourself.

Establish face-to-face relationships with trustworthy friends and relatives. People who have experienced terrible breakups or divorces can be especially helpful. They can comfort you by saying that healing and making new relationships are possible since they know how you feel. Regular face-to-face encounters might help you recover after a breakup and regain equilibrium in your life.

Spend time with people who inspire, value, and encourage you. Select carefully who you get in touch with. Spend time with positive people who will truly listen to you. It's critical that you can be open and honest about what you're going through without fear of judgment, condemnation, or advice on what to do.

Obtain outside help if you require it. Should you find it difficult to assist others? The most important component is having at least one place where you feel comfortable speaking candidly.

Create new connections. If you believe that your social network has diminished due to the divorce or breakup, try trying to meet new individuals. Attend a course, become involved in neighborhood activities, join a networking group or a club related to your field of interest, or volunteer at a local school, house of worship, or other organization.

Taking Care of Oneself After a Breakup

Divorce is a very traumatic and life-changing event. When going through a challenging emotional period or a big life transition, you must take time to take care of yourself. The strain and turmoil of a significant breakup might make you more vulnerable both mentally and physically.

Treat yourself well as you get over the sickness. Get enough sleep, try to reduce your workload, and attempt to remove any additional stressors from your life. One of the most crucial things you can learn after a breakup is how to look after yourself. As you come to terms with your loss and begin to draw lessons from it, you may decide to go forward with taking better care of yourself and making informed decisions.

Self-Care Guidelines

Every day, give yourself some time. Set aside time each day for relaxing and peaceful pursuits to help you heal. Enjoy a nice cup of tea, walk in the park, listen to music, take a hot bath, massage, read your favorite book, go to yoga, or just spend time with close friends.

Always be conscious of your needs and express them to others by speaking out. Respect what you believe is right and best for you, even if it's not what your ex or other people want. To honor what is right for you, say "no" without feeling guilty or nervous.

Follow a timetable. Divorce or separation can completely upend your life, exacerbating feelings of worry, doubt, and bewilderment. Resuming a regular schedule can provide a soothing sense of order and normalcy.

To improve your ability to think clearly, try delaying making decisions until you feel less emotional.

Never turn to alcohol, drugs, or food for solace. When you're going through a breakup, you could find yourself wanting to take all the pain and isolation away from yourself. However, using food, medicine, or drink as a crutch has negative long-term effects. Developing healthier coping strategies for negative emotions is essential.

Find New Areas of Interest. Divorce or separation signifies a new beginning as well as an end. Seize the opportunity to explore novel interests and activities. Rather than living in the past and regretting it, you can live in the present by doing fun, new things.

Making Wise Choices: Eating Properly, Sleeping Enough, and Working Out

It's easy to overlook healthy habits when stressed out after a split or divorce. You can find yourself underindulging in or overindulging in your favorite junk food. Exercise may be harder to fit in, and sleep may be harder because of the increasing duties at home. However, all of your hard work to progress towards a better life would be in vain if you don't adopt a long-term healthy lifestyle.

First chapter: Pause, consider!

Take a moment to reflect.

You want your ex back, that's why.

There isn't another course of action. You realize you want your ex back and aren't ready to end the relationship. You want to give your supposed soul mate and love story another go. That is the reason you initially purchased this book.

It's time to go on your quest to find your lost love. Though "lost" may be a strong phrase, how about "paused love" that you want to rekindle? Yes, that is what we will do.

The narrative is the same: you realize you will stop at nothing to get your ex back into your life. And by anything, I mean anything that would be in a romance movie.

However, you must first determine whether it's proper before standing outside their window with a jukebox or paying someone to conduct a flash mob to your theme song.

Admittedly, we've all been sidetracked by our emotions, and love occasionally clouds our judgment. You must first consider the reasons behind the breakup in the first place. It matters why rather than who did what or who broke up with whom.

What caused your breakup? Was there a fight as a reason? Has there been any cheating? If it was for "irreconcilable differences"—as most Hollywood actors would say—or something else entirely, the cause is crucial in determining if you should reconcile with your ex.

Let me just clarify before we continue: if the relationship was poisonous and abusive, you shouldn't enter into it again. Simply let it go if you are the one being mistreated. Recall my statement that our emotions often override our judgments. Well, you can't allow it to prevail. Furthermore, it's advisable to go on and get counseling if you're on the other side of the curtain and feel some sort of regret for whatever you did.

You also need to think about if the other person shares your feelings. Sadly, just because you believe a reunion is in order doesn't mean they agree.

This book is for when you think they might still love you. Additionally, there's a chance that they're over you entirely. Maybe you don't enjoy them as much as you used to. Sometimes, it's necessary to acknowledge their emotions and let them go. It's hard to revive a romantic relationship with someone who isn't interested in spending time with you again, and it's rude to try to make someone do something they don't want to do.

Just keep in mind that you are a person who cares about this individual and that you want the best for them, even when it's not involving you. "Being romantic" and "pressuring someone into something they don't want" are two very different things.

Thus, do not do the latter if you are considering doing so.

Keep in mind the point this chapter is attempting to make.

Recall that you want them back, not for them to despise you. Consider what your true desires are. Is it truly your desire to have them back in your life? Remember that missing someone and your possessions does not equate to continuing to feel feelings for them. So, find out how the two differ from one another.

No, I'm not straying from the subject. I'm right on target, just at the subject's earliest and most important phase.

The fact remains that romance is wonderful and all, which is this book's main theme. Rekindling love is the main goal of this novel.

Creating a poisonous environment between two people is not the purpose of this book, though.

Therefore, you must think about what I outlined before trying to accomplish anything.

I know you're asking why this is in the book's first chapter rather than an afterthought in the last chapter. This is a crucial matter that should come first because it isn't something to consider afterward.

Now that we have that out let's get to the exciting part!

After you've realized that, try to win them back by sweeping them off their feet.

That is, after all, the purpose of this book.

It's normal for your kids to ask questions in response, and you should honestly answer them to help them process the information. "Who will live in the house?" "Will I have to move or change schools?" "May I ever see my friends again?" and "May I ever decide who I live with?" are just a few of the questions your children may have asked. Try to be dependable and attentive when answering their questions. For your children to comprehend the separation, respond reassuringly and transparently.

You may say to your children, "For the present, Mother will reside in the house. You will all remain with her and Father will visit at the end of the week or you will go visit him at the end of the week. We will share a great deal of the everyday requirements until the separation is settled."

You might also include a special event your children participate in, such as a tournament or birthday party. You may add, "We have decided that Mother will pick you up from Stephanie's party on Sunday," or, "We will both be at your competition on Friday to support you."

Prepare for your children to react in a way close to home. They may react to the separation in various ways, ranging from shock to outrage to disarray to coercion. Recognize that your children may have significant response strengths, and try to meet their needs. You may also be experiencing significant emotions, so supporting your children may help you adjust to the separation.

Younger children may react to the separation by reverting to behaviors they had outgrown, such as thumb-sucking or wetting the bed. Older children may react with a mixture of fury, anxiety, and despair. They may also become disheartened and detached.

Be a decent audience. You can help your children weather the storm of the separation by being both a decent audience and a decent parent. Your children may need you to be available to attend to their interests and concerns regarding the separation, so sit down with them and pay attention to what they have to say. When tuning in, try not to interrupt your children while they are speaking. Instead, show open nonverbal communication by staying nearby, keeping your arms relaxed by your sides, and turning your body to face your children.

You can ask your children questions and offer them comfort when needed. Try not to try to answer all of their questions or concerns. If you are unsure how to respond, you can say, "I don't know how to address your inquiry, but rather, I realize that I will constantly be hanging around for you and that I love you." My love for you remains unchanged despite our being apart.

Talk to the people who matter most. You should inform other influential adults in your children's lives about your separation. Then, as your children go about their regular activities around you, these role models can watch them. You can receive updates on your children's progress and learn whether there are any concerns regarding how your children are acting due to the separation.

You might tell these influential people, "My accomplice and I were isolated. I'm stressed over what it could mean for the kids. I realize this will be a troublesome time for them. How about you tell me whether there are any issues with the kids in the next few weeks or months?"

Maintain consistent routines and habits. Establishing consistent routines and habits for your children will help them find comfort in the familiar and help them adjust to the change. Knowing what to expect gives most children a strong sense of security and assurance, especially during a chaotic time. You and your partner should agree upon a daily routine or schedule to share with the children. In this sense, the children perceive that they are both solid and aware of what lies ahead daily.

Even though your children will now live in different households due to the split, you still need to maintain the same training habits. You and your partner should maintain the same rules, incentives, and expectations for your children to feel stable and consistent. The established rules should not be bent or altered for your children by you or your partner, as this may confuse or enrage them.

Treat your prior partnership with respect. Avoid having serious conversations about your ex-partner in front of your children since this might increase stress and strain. If you find it bothersome, like you did with your former partner, you should focus on simply being courteous and respectful of the kids.

Avoid arguing or fighting with your former partner in front of the children, as this will make them resentful. You must demonstrate to your children that even if you don't live together, you and your ex-partner can still be reliable, helpful parents. Your children are pawns or messengers between you and your ex-partner. This may encourage your children to study more difficult subjects and put further strain on the entire family.

Obtain professional assistance for your children. If your children seem to be struggling with the separation and you do not have the tools necessary to support them, you may want to consider taking them to a counselor or expert. Some children require expert guidance and support to adjust to the separation and become well-adjusted adults.

You may look for a professional who works closely with children or a mentor who understands how children cope with division and separation. Additionally, you might need support or therapy while working through the separation. Seeking professional help will help you support your children and be there for them during this difficult time more easily.

Allow your children to maintain relationships with past relatives. Even when you and your ex-partner are no longer together, your children won't automatically cut off contact with all of their former family members. You should make an effort to encourage your children to continue their relationships with your ex's family and close friends, as this will provide them with a sense of security and comfort. You should let your children spend time with long-term friends and family. Additionally, you should try using the same babysitters or childcare providers you did before the breakup.

Encouraging your children to maintain relationships with people in their lives before the separation will ensure that they have a stable support system. This will help your children become responsible adults and cope with the difficulties of being apart from you.

Complete other financial agreements and child support payments. Throughout the divorce, you and your partner will most likely reach an agreement about child support. Make sure you complete your funds and that your partner does as well. This will ensure less conflict between you and your children and that you are not drawn into arguments over money.

If you and your partner dislike child support payments and other financial arrangements in general, you should discuss them privately and alone. Avoid bringing your children into the discussion or using them as pawns in a dispute. This will only foster increased pressure and a strong inclination.

Provide a stable, stable environment for your children. Even though you aren't together right now, you and your ex should still give your utmost to be excellent parents to your children. Make an effort to provide your children with a stable and intelligent environment at home. To help your children and offer support, you must ensure you take care of your needs and stay well.

You should maintain a regular workout schedule and a healthy diet. Additionally, you should schedule time for self-care and make sure your needs are satisfied. You should also visit your loved ones and be social. When you truly need it, they can support you support you, ensuring you can raise your children.

Start by examining any potential partners with your children. If and when you decide to go back on dates, you should consider your children. Take your time and go cautiously; you don't want to abruptly jump into a new relationship and upset your children. If you begin dating seriously, you should talk to your children about your current situation. To make them feel included, let them know you believe you are ready to go on and keep them updated.

Letting your children know if and when you decide to move in with someone else is also important. These decisions may upset your kids, especially if they occur soon after the divorce. Before moving further, talk about them and listen to their points of view.

Find a network of emotionally supportive people. To help you through difficult times, you should also look for emotionally supporting networks for yourself and your children.

Having emotionally supporting networks can help relieve any pressure or stress during a difficult time for all involved parties during a separation.

You should get your rest from knowledgeable, emotionally supportive networks such as advisors and experts. Perhaps you decide to deal with your children and see an expert one-on-one. Private emotional support networks, such as close friends or family, can also be a place to rest. To help your children feel supported, you could decide to have a family dinner with family members or decide to eat alone with friends one night a week.

## SUPPOSE IT ISN'T AMICABLE?

Breakups are rarely beneficial. Despite your best efforts to stay friends, most breakups end badly. It might have occurred during a severe argument, possibly with some sobbing and yelling. If that's the case, you can't start messaging him/her again and assume that everything has been forgotten. The advice given here won't work; therefore, you'll need to develop a fresh strategy to win him or her back.

Allowing the Fury to Dim

Likely, folks are still experiencing negative emotional highs following a harsh breakup. This indicates that they are still experiencing feelings of rage, perplexity, and resentment over the situation. Reconciliation is never something you should try while your ex is still displaying these kinds of feelings.

More significantly, you should confirm that these feelings have left your mind. It's critical that you were able to get past it and maintain composure. You can only address the problem appropriately and achieve your desired outcomes in this manner.

How much longer will your ex be enraged? Since there is no set time frame, nobody can be certain. Generally speaking, it differs from person to person, but you make a solid foundation. They are likely in the same predicament if you're still not thrilled.

Presenting Closure

Without closure, you could never make amends with your former partner. Closure is likely reached if you and your ex parted as "good" friends; all you need to do now is take it from there. Even though these relationships ended horribly, you both need this closure to go on. Your objective during closure should be to formally terminate the previous relationship rather than to start a new one.

Most people find it difficult to bring closure to a relationship that has ended, particularly if there has been no communication. There's no other way to do this; you must message the other person to discuss things and formalize the agreement.

To finish the relationship better, you could send them an SMS requesting a private meeting. You made a wise decision by doing this, as it gives the impression that you are the more experienced partner. It would be difficult for your ex to reject this kind of request.

Launching Your Initiative

It's time to start organizing your campaign to get your ex back after a successful closure. As the book's earlier section indicates, you must wait for you and your ex to get over the breakup. What you should be doing right now is getting ready for what is ahead.

It will take time to get your ex back, so be prepared to dedicate months or perhaps a year to the effort. It's important to remember that you will be going through changes following the breakup, so getting used to things before trying something new is preferable.

Using Technology to Reunite with Your Ex

You could use a computer or a cell phone to get in touch with your ex. This strategy is helpful, particularly if you and your ex don't regularly get together. For example, you probably can't send them "physical signals" anymore if your social circles have suddenly become polarised. Getting noticed is guaranteed when you send them an SMS.

Utilizing Your Phone

It's advisable to start with a lighthearted text message. It's not necessary to confront them directly and demand a reconciliation. Alternatively, you might just say "Hi" or send a smiley or a quote to see how they're doing. A "soft entry" would indicate whether the other person is comfortable communicating with you. The next step after sending the first message is to just wait for a response. This may be the most stressful part, particularly if you don't hear back immediately. The benefit of texting your ex is that it gives them more time to consider how to respond. Because it doesn't seem "urgent," unlike a call, it seems more friendly to your ex.

Increasing communication with your ex is the first step towards texting your ex back. A weekly text message with a quote or a simple "hi" might be the ideal place to start. Getting your ex to respond to even one of your texts is your aim here. Don't send them too many texts, but get them used to the idea that you're reaching out again.

Engage them in extended chats only once you've seen a consistent pattern of them responding or starting texts. Take it slow and question them about their present activities and how they've been. Discovering the nature of their social life can help you decide whether to invite yourself or your former partner to meet up informally.

Making Use of the Internet

The wonderful thing about making contact via the internet is that you can watch first before taking any action. WordPress, Pinterest, and others can assist you with this effort. By looking through her profiles, you can determine whether he or she is in a relationship and whether you two still have a chance. This is crucial because you DO NOT want to sour any current relationships she may be in.

This should be extremely simple to find if you follow her blog or are a friend on Facebook. You should also use this opportunity to ascertain his or her emotional state. Do you believe unresolved issues between you and your ex have not been resolved after the breakup? Understanding their emotional state would help you determine the best action for a reconciliation.

The same strategy that works for text messaging also applies to using the internet to mend fences with your former partner. You can accomplish this by tagging them in images, videos, and articles you know they enjoy or by sending them a lighthearted personal greeting. This is a nice approach to start a casual discussion. When determining whether your ex is open to a reconciliation, even something as easy as clicking "like" on their posts should get you started. But what if they have barred you? It hints that your ex isn't ready for a reconciliation when they block you. You might want to check frequently to find out if you've been removed from their prohibited list. You can attempt to start a conversation with them in the interim by using alternative communication channels.

## WAYS TO MAKE YOUR RELATIONSHIP BETTER

Looking back at my relationship experience with Liz, I realized that I never wanted to end things with her again once I played my cards well and won her back. At that moment, I saw I needed to do more for her and take the steps to strengthen our connection.

One of our strongest desires is to be in a loving relationship. Intimate relationships enhance our sense of intimacy and our sense of connectedness to the world at large. We feel profound fulfillment and satisfaction when our hearts are full of love. We grow in kindness, generosity, and tolerance.

But personal intimacy affects us in ways that go beyond our feelings. Many scientific studies have shown that the power of love directly affects our physical and emotional well-being by strengthening our immune systems, improving cardiovascular health, and extending our life spans.

These five steps can help you keep the spark alive and grow in your relationship with your spouse without breaking up.

Make Friends.

Any successful relationship needs a solid base of friendship. Think about showing your spouse the same consideration, decency, and respect as you would a close friend. Help, hear, and laugh together. Never give in to the need to behave impolitely or rudely.

Maintain your sense of self.

The needs of each partner as an individual must be balanced with the demands of the relationship. Conversely, you don't want people's emotional separations to be excessively wide. If you're not with each other, you emotionally retreat. On the other hand, when a couple depends too much on one another, they lose their sense of identity. You two should be at just the right distance for closeness while retaining your identities. Don't be afraid to pursue interests and relationships outside of your relationship.

Take Action

Physical proximity is a healthy and natural extension of a relationship. But our best sexual intentions are often set to rest as we collapse into a tired heap at the end of the day. Rather, you both need to decide to step up the intensity of your relationship. Put the dishes in the sink, turn off the laptop, and go to work! Set the mood by burning scented candles or incense and playing seductive music to encourage relaxation. Look for ways to use touch to communicate your loving energy.

Honor each other.

Giving your partner praise and demonstrating affection for them should become a daily practice. Loving thoughts bring you closer together by assisting you in remembering each other's best traits. Don't be shy about expressing your love and affection for your mate; let them know how much they mean to you.

Put up a valiant defense.

Disagreements and arguments will certainly arise; therefore, how you debate matters more than whether you argue at all. When disputes come up, try to keep them to a minimum. Please give me ten minutes. After ten minutes, it gets tedious. Also, keep the conversation in check. Remain on topic and refrain from discussing things that happened a week or month ago.

Think back to the beginning to determine the solution.

In nearly every breakup, remembering when your relationship started is the secret to getting your ex back.

How did your partner behave when you first met them? What's more, how did you act when you initially started dating?

Most likely, you were both acting appropriately. You both worked hard to ensure the other person had a good time.

Furthermore, you would have been driven to make a good impression on the other person and disregarded any small behavioral or personality defects. Now, think back to your last conversation with your former partner. Did the two of you have a good interaction? Or did you quarrel, experience tension, anger, or worry about the other person's thoughts?

If your ex and you were not getting along, chances are good that this person's mental picture of you is one in which you are fighting, upset, sobbing, and anxious about the relationship's future. In this circumstance, it is not feasible to think of joyful ideas about a bright and happy future together. Rather, they're probably thinking about how to meet someone who resembles the person they initially saw you as.

Yes, you, as you were the first time you met. He or she would have fallen in love with the joyful, confident, positive, energetic, independent person you were when you first met. You would have made him or her feel good while they were with you, and they would have liked to wonder when you would find time in your busy schedule to visit them again. What then changed?

Mistakes You Could Have Done

Do you find yourself begging your ex to get back together even after they've broken up with you? Yes, you know this is the person you were supposed to spend the rest of your life with, even though your heart may be breaking. Does your ex, however, feel the same way?

If you've made an effort to persuade your ex that you're the ideal person for them through messages, emails, texts, or phone calls, chances are

You're displacing them even further. Your frequent attempts to contact your ex are seen by her as harassing behavior, which is the problem.

You're moving too quickly. No one, man or woman, likes to be in a desperate situation. It radiates clinginess and insecurity, which are incredibly bad for anyone.

Both men and women find the confidence of the other sex to be quite attractive. A confident individual who understands their needs and desires

Everyone finds it quite enticing to have things done for them by someone else. However, someone who suddenly becomes adamant that committing to you is the only way they can achieve happiness is suddenly quite unattractive. Remember that the person you fell in love with was likely a happier, more confident, more lively version of you. Your ex may wonder what happened to the person they fell in love with because you're not quite the same wretched, lonely, desperate person you once were.

Ultimately, the unhappy person in front of them Their current feelings are not the same as their initial feelings of love. Would you think you were spending time with a terrific person if all you heard were grievances, disagreements, begging, pleading, and fruitless attempts at reconciliation?

Persuasive every single time you interacted with that individual?

Not; you would rather hang out with someone a little more entertaining, wouldn't you?

What, then, should you do if you have already made the mistake of further alienating your ex by begging or even pleading with them to get back to you? That's what we'll discuss next because, despite your habit of incessantly phoning, texting, emailing, or messaging your ex, there may still be hope for you to repair your damaged relationship.

## Reversing Earlier Issues

The first step to getting your ex back, no matter how much you'd like to, is to stop communicating with them. Give up texting. Give up making calls. Give up sending emails. Just stop talking about them; don't ask his or her buddies about them.

Now, think back to who you were before the meeting. Everything in your life was likely going well. You would have been independent regarding employment, friends, and hobbies. Rekindle their passion the way it did before you met your ex.

Don't do it, even if your low emotional condition makes you want to remain home and wait for the phone to ring, and you don't feel like it. All you need is a smile and some time spent with those you love. Spend time with people who give you confidence in your identity and work.

Clear any negative acquaintances or companions that could inspire you to dwell in your heartbreak. You should stay away from them since they will not help you win your ex back. It's critical to awaken your confident, independent side that initially drew your ex.

Your ex will eventually become concerned about you and wonder why you haven't phoned or contacted them. You won't be there yet, but you will have come a long way by this time. Consider this: your ex's concern suggests they still feel something for you.

The most important lesson is to quit talking to them and concentrate on your inner journey.

Eliminating the Fairytale Relationship Stereotype

Hollywood films are mostly responsible for most people's romantic, fairytale views of love. Thanks to the silver screen, we've been taught to believe that, after much drama, struggle, and backbiting, the love of our lives will suddenly realize their mistake, and we'll all live happily ever after.

Idealistic romantic films are more likely to show this happening than real life, even though it isn't realistic.

Is it true that your ex isn't the key to your happiness? You are, indeed.

You can still be happy and fulfilled without another person in your life. You just need yourself and the things that ultimately bring you joy, such as your hobbies, passions, and areas of personal interest.

You were probably already confident, independent, and content when you first met your ex. The opposite sex finds these characteristics highly attractive. Thus, depart.

Enjoy yourself. Spend time with your buddies. Watch lighthearted comedies that won't offend you or provoke thought. Invest in new clothes. Obtain a fresh haircut. Get some exercise. Take some time to pamper and groom yourself.

When you look good, you feel good; when you feel good, you become attractive to everyone around you again. Your confidence will come back effortlessly, and you'll find something to smile about every corner you turn.

There's more rationale for this tactic.

Reconnecting with the person you were when your ex first saw you and fell in love with you can enable you to move on from your breakup with them and get over it.

You'll start to feel better about yourself when you've taken some time to get your confidence back to where it was before meeting your ex.

You'll also be far more ready to see your former partner again.

## THE TIMING IS CRUCIAL.

When you and your ex can discuss what went wrong in your relationship honestly, you'll know the timing is appropriate. This allows you to jointly decide on the direction you wish to take your relationship.

Reuniting signifies a willingness on both sides to address the issues and acknowledge your shared responsibility. It might be time for coffee if you have stayed in touch via text or email. Feel free to be informal and lighthearted. Reconnect and get to know each other. If one of you starts to feel uncomfortable, call it quits for now and catch up later.

Rekindling this informal friendship is one way to pave the way for future ones. Remain composed and avoid pressing the issue if your former partner has consented to a casual encounter. If you want your ex back, you must accept that timing is crucial.

The 7-Step Plan for Reuniting With Your Ex

1. Give up assigning blame.
It is pointless to assign blame any longer. There have been errors committed and irreversible actions taken. Moving on and accepting the circumstance as it is is your only option.

2. Remain Active
Continue doing the activities you find enjoyable. Your former partner won't find you attractive if you start feeling down and sluggish. Although it's difficult, doing this will prevent you from always dwelling on your split.

3. Be Truthful

Recall that relationships require effort. No relationship develops naturally on its own. As two distinct people, you both have your own needs and desires. Don't compromise who you are to appease your spouse. In actuality, it alienates people over time. There will always be disagreements, but that doesn't mean a great relationship has to suffer because of them.

4. Don't Ask or Suggest

Begging and pleading for your ex to take you back is the best way to ruin your self-esteem. Prove to them that to rebuild your connection, you are unwilling to compromise your integrity or your identity. It turns out that this works well. It lets your ex know you care, but you won't take it further than begging or asking them to return.

5. Make Use of Your Knowledge

You are aware that nothing can return to how it was. Your ex is more likely to open up and want to chat if you can own up to your faults and make an effort to make amends. When conversing, avoid the pitfall of engaging in a dispute. Acknowledge and steer clear of the behavioral patterns that led to those conflicts. You and your former partner can only resolve issues and behave like responsible adults in this manner.

6. Exercise patience

Recall that your relationship's breakdown happened gradually. It will take time to repair the harm. It's also important to give the feelings enough time to subside. Most couples stay away from one another for a few weeks or more. Remain true to this and resist letting your feelings overwhelm you. Being patient is a far better option than losing hope of reuniting with your former partner.

Be the person who captivates their heart.
Recall the things that used to bring your ex joy. After dating for some time, did you cease doing such things? Doing the activities that first made your ex fall in love with you is one of the best strategies to get them back. Use the fact that your ex was once drawn to and enchanted by you to rekindle your connection.

Chapter 5: Avoid Creating Jealousy with Your Ex

People today tend to see love as a psychological game, which is a problem. Specific stimuli can cause comparable responses. Usually, the goal is to elicit the desired response, but this is a simple solution that will inevitably backfire.
During a breakup, you may find yourself desperate enough to turn to unscrupulous

methods. Begging is a desperate enough tactic, even though we can only regard it as a pitiful means of winning back your ex. However, there is more to making your ex jealous than sheer desperation. It is merely an insensitive deed.

We've now covered why you must resist the urge to get in touch with your former partner. However, as long as you agree to cool things off and think about getting back together, this is OK.

You must keep up the momentum that this phase is building towards a reunion. You will never make any progress if you make your ex jealous.

Make an Emotional Appeal

It's possible that your ex still feels something for you. Even though there may have been misunderstandings that led to the breakup, your connection is still intact. Consider the breakup a time to "cool down" and allow yourself to control your emotions.

There is just so much you can do to hurt someone by making your ex envious. Suppose your former partner is optimistic about your reunion, only to discover on Facebook that there are pictures of you in a private selfie with someone else. And just ten days have passed since the breakup!

It's wise to never presume that your former partner is emotionless.

Never Seize the Opportunity

Courting someone from your ex's social group is one definite method to end things with them completely.

More foolish than that, what could be?

This is an action that will only serve to sever friendships. Why put yourself through the hassle of ending two things simultaneously when your relationship is already problematic?

The idea is to never take advantage of someone to further your disgrace or to make a statement to your former partner.

An Indiscriminate Symptom

Having someone step in temporarily shows insensitivity and indifference, which exacerbates the situation. It demonstrates your lack of concern for your ex's feelings or the purpose of the relationship for either of you.

Intimate forms of love are important affairs whose customs ought to be honored proportionately as partners honor one another. Please handle the breakup maturely if you truly love your ex and your heart yearns for such affection. Tell your ex that you can be the person who is ready to take ownership of your actions and take this relationship to new heights.

Face love with an adult perspective rather than that of a youngster who sees things as toys that may be played with.

## Chapter 6: Vanish for Thirty Days

In the past, we defined a breakup as a situation in which you and your former partner don't communicate. It's a time to step back and consider certain choices and routines. It's also a chance to let things settle for a moment.

As a general rule, neither of you must get in touch with the other directly following the breakup. This simply means that, while feelings are raw and scars are visible, you must stay away from one another for as little as thirty days.

You must, therefore, learn to be more withdrawn by minimizing your online presence, spending time alone, and resisting the need to text or speak.

You can see that this could be a very challenging task.

However, if getting him or her back is essential to you, then you want to think about the following:

Absence of Communication

To reiterate, you must ignore the itch, regardless of its intensity.

Refrain from texting or chatting with your ex, especially in the early days after the breakup. However, some people frequently disobey this guideline.

Since the two of you are still in shock over that stressful moment when the split was revealed, there's no need to contact our ex. Neither of you knows how the other handles the breakup, and emotions are still high.

Attempting to communicate with your ex too soon will simply make you feel awkward. You can't even try texting or calling them.

It is that feeling when you are at a loss for words and attempt to maintain your relationship with your ex as "just a friend." Who, though, in their right mind would do that? It's also important to remember that getting in touch with your ex too soon can only mean you're prepared to move on. Saying "Hi" merely indicates that you've come to terms with the breakup and are over the experience. But that's not what we're talking about here.

You recognize that there is still a chance for the relationship to succeed again and that you still feel the same affection for him or her.

You should think about talking to your ex for 30 days if you know how you feel. Though it may sting, over time, it can be beneficial.

Steer clear of Facebook.

Regardless of location, social media can strengthen relationships between people.

You are coping with emotional distance in your breakup experience, which requires many risks to overcome.

Just as you should resist the want to contact, text, or chat with your ex, you should never think that finding out if they are online or tracking them will make things easier or much less frantic.

Maintain a Journal

Keep a notepad where you may record your thoughts and the evolution of the breakup to help you deal with the lack of communication. In this manner, you might let go of your feelings about the breakup without exceeding the 30-day limit.

www.ingramcontent.com/pod-product-compliance
Lightning Source LLC
Chambersburg PA
CBHW052150110526
44591CB00012B/1922